...IF YOU TRAVELED ON
The Underground Railroad

by Ellen Levine

illustrated by Larry Johnson

SCHOLASTIC INC.

New York Toronto London Auckland Sydney
Mexico City New Delhi Hong Kong Buenos Aires

In memory of those who escaped and those who helped them.

With grateful acknowledgement to Dr. Martin Duberman, Professor of History, Herbert H. Lehman College,
City University of New York, for his thoughtful review of the manuscript;
and special thanks to Mada Liebman for introducing me to the remarkable records
of the Underground Railroad kept by William Still and originally published in 1872.

ISBN 0-439-81474-X

12 11 10 9 8 7 6 5 4 3 2 1   6 7 8 9 10 11/0

Printed in the U.S.A.   23

A note to the reader about slavery

It is a sad fact that throughout history almost every society at one time or another has had slaves. There were slaves in the Middle East, Asia, Africa, Europe, and North and South America.

From 1502 to 1870, it's believed some 11 million Africans were taken from their homes and sold as slaves in countries across the Atlantic Ocean. Most of them went to Brazil and the Caribbean. Half a million men, women, and children from Africa were brought to what is now the United States. These slaves had children who also became slaves. As the years passed, there were more and more slaves in the country. By the time the United States became a nation in 1783, most people who were slaves had been born here.

In 1808, the United States government made a law against bringing in any more slaves from other countries. But it was still legal to buy slaves within the country for another 57 years.

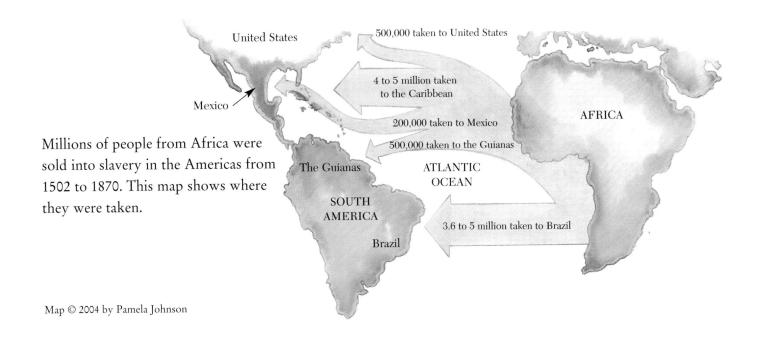

Millions of people from Africa were sold into slavery in the Americas from 1502 to 1870. This map shows where they were taken.

United States

500,000 taken to United States

4 to 5 million taken to the Caribbean

Mexico

200,000 taken to Mexico

500,000 taken to the Guianas

AFRICA

The Guianas

ATLANTIC OCEAN

SOUTH AMERICA

Brazil

3.6 to 5 million taken to Brazil

Introduction   7

What was the Underground Railroad?   8

How did the Underground Railroad get its name?   10

When did the Underground Railroad start running?   12

What did it mean to be a slave?   14

Could you buy yourself?   19

Why would you run away?   20

Where would you first go when you ran away?   23

What dangers did you face?   24

What would you eat while you were hiding?   25

Where was the safest place to go?   26

How would you hear about Canada?   28

How did owners try to catch the fugitives?   29

Did anyone help the owners?   31

Would you use disguises when you ran away?   32

Did you use special signals and codes on the
Underground Railroad?   36

How would you trick the slave hunters?   40

Were there special hiding places on the
    Underground Railroad?   42

How long would you stay at a station?   44

How long would the whole trip take?   46

When was the best time of year to escape?   47

Who worked on the Underground Railroad?   49

How did people learn about the Underground
    Railroad?   52

Was everyone in the North against slavery?   54

How many slaves escaped?   56

What happened if you were caught?   57

Were people who helped you punished?   58

What did the Presidents of the United States think
    about the Underground Railroad?   59

What would you do when you became free?   60

When did the Underground Railroad stop running?   63

Places to Visit   64

Introduction

Before 1860 there were about four million slaves in America. They lived and worked in the South. Most of them wanted to escape to the North, to freedom. And thousands of them did.

From the very beginning of American history, slaves fled from their owners. They were called fugitives. The great majority of fugitive slaves ran away between 1830 and 1860. They traveled on the most famous "road" of the day — the Underground Railroad.

There were great dangers for those who traveled this way, as well as for those who helped them.

This book is about this mysterious railroad — how it worked, who rode on it, and why its very name meant freedom.

What was the Underground Railroad?

The Underground Railroad wasn't a real railroad. It was the secret way to get from the South and slavery to the North and freedom. Sometimes you would ride on a real railroad, sometimes in a horse-drawn cart, sometimes in a fancy carriage, sometimes on a boat, sometimes on horseback. And much of the time you would walk. The whole trip was called the Underground Railroad.

When you traveled in this secret way, you stayed at special hiding places throughout the South and North. Often you had to find your own hiding places. Other times people hid you until you could travel on.

The houses the slaves hid in along the way were called "stations." People who helped the fugitives were called "railroad workers." Some were "conductors" — they would lead you to the next station. Others were "station masters" — they would feed you and give you a place to sleep until you left for the next station.

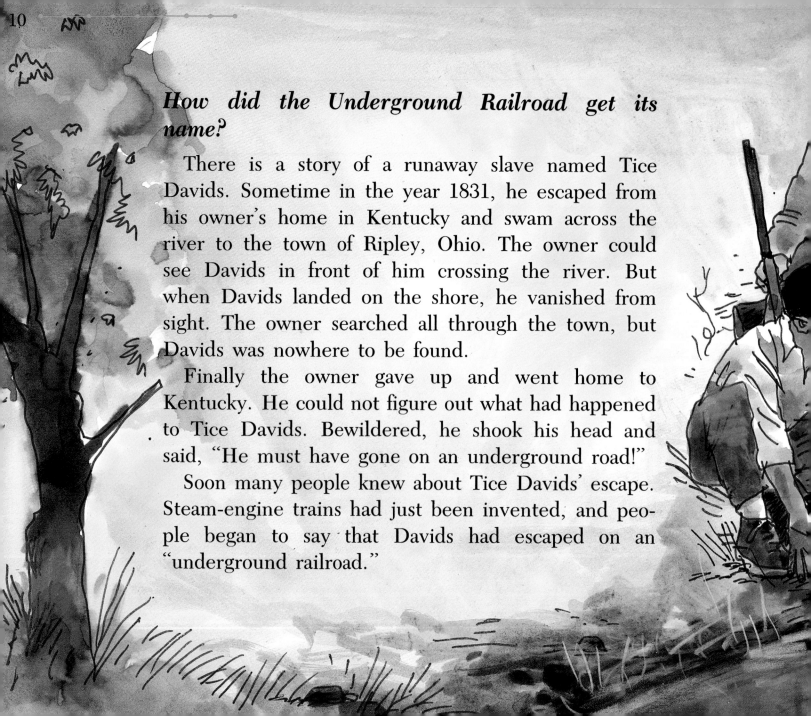

How did the Underground Railroad get its name?

There is a story of a runaway slave named Tice Davids. Sometime in the year 1831, he escaped from his owner's home in Kentucky and swam across the river to the town of Ripley, Ohio. The owner could see Davids in front of him crossing the river. But when Davids landed on the shore, he vanished from sight. The owner searched all through the town, but Davids was nowhere to be found.

Finally the owner gave up and went home to Kentucky. He could not figure out what had happened to Tice Davids. Bewildered, he shook his head and said, "He must have gone on an underground road!"

Soon many people knew about Tice Davids' escape. Steam-engine trains had just been invented, and people began to say that Davids had escaped on an "underground railroad."

The name stuck. And from then on, whenever slaves escaped, people said they had traveled on the Underground Railroad.

It was a perfect name — "underground" because it was secret and you couldn't see it, and "railroad" because it seemed to run regularly and swiftly.

When did the Underground Railroad start running?

The first slaves were brought to America in 1619. And there were escapes from then on. The Underground Railroad didn't get its name until the 1800s, but whatever people called it, there were slaves who ran away from their owners to live in freedom.

Some escaped into the forests and swamps of Florida to live with the Seminole Indians. Others ran away to live in the part of America ruled by Spain, or to the northern states, where slavery was not allowed.

Some slaves even ran away to fight on the side of the British during the American Revolutionary War. The British promised them freedom. The Americans made no promises. That's why some blacks said that July 4th was not their Independence Day. And as long as there was slavery in America, they were right.

What did it mean to be a slave?

To be a slave meant that you had nothing you could call your own — not even your name. You, the clothes you wore, the food you ate, the place you slept, all belonged to another person. That person was your owner. And just to make sure you didn't forget it, your last name was often the same as your owner's.

To be a slave meant that you had to do whatever work your owner wanted. Some slaves worked from before sunrise until after dark in the rice or cotton or bean fields. Others worked in the owner's house.

Sometimes owners sent slaves to work for other people who paid the slaves. Of course, the owner kept most of the money. The slaves were given just enough to live on. Even so, a few were able to save a little money.

To be a slave meant that your owner could punish you whenever he or she wanted to. One slave was beaten because he called his owner "Mister" instead of "Master." Another was whipped because he had looked at a slave the master had beaten to death, and cried.

To be a slave meant that you had to have your owner's permission to do almost anything. You couldn't walk down the road without a pass from your owner saying it was okay for you to be there. You couldn't visit anyone without a pass. If you didn't have a pass, you could be arrested, whipped, and put in jail until your owner came to get you.

One of the worst things about being a slave was that you could be sold — like a cow or a pig or a piece of furniture. Many white people believed they had a right to own black people. If you own something, you can sell it. And so if your owner needed money, he might sell you to a slave trader. These traders went around to different owners and bought slaves. Then they would sell them to other people.

At the markets, many slaves were put on sale at the same time. People would come up to you and open your mouth to see if your teeth were healthy. They would pinch your arms and legs to see if you were strong. They would make you bend this way and that way to see if anything was wrong with you.

To be a slave meant you probably didn't know how to read and write. In many southern states, whites who taught blacks how to read could be fined and put in jail. Blacks who taught other slaves might be whipped and put in jail. If you learned, you did it secretly.

Today everybody goes to school. Why do you think that slave owners were so afraid that the slaves would learn to read and write?

Could you buy yourself?

Sometimes. If you had saved enough money, your master might sell you to yourself. Then he would give you "free papers." These said that no one owned you. You were a free person.

A few owners let their slaves buy themselves. Most said, "Absolutely not." And others took the money and then refused to write the free papers. If that happened to you, there would be nothing you could do.

One slave ran away from his owner and lived in Massachusetts, where he got a job and worked hard. After a few years he saved up some money and sent it to the owner. He said that since the man had once owned him, he thought it was fair to pay him.

Other people disagreed with that. They said it was wrong to have slaves. They said it was wrong for anyone to pay money to be free. They said *everybody* had a right to be free.

Why would you run away?

Many slaves ran away because they were about to be sold. Sometimes an owner needed money, and so he or she decided to sell a few slaves. Or you might be sold if your owner died.

Everyone was afraid of being sold to owners who lived in Georgia and Alabama. All slaves had heard stories about the terrible rice and cotton plantations down there:

— about how you worked all day and sometimes all night,

— about how you might be chained at night to keep you from running away,

— about how some owners made you work so hard you got sick and died. Then they bought new slaves and started all over.

Many slave families were separated when a parent or child was sold. You might grow up hearing about brothers and sisters you had never met — brothers and sisters who had been sold before you were born.

Some slaves ran away because their owners beat them. Others ran because of broken promises. They had been told they would be free when the owner died. But the owner's relatives cheated. They lied and said that the owner had never promised to free anyone.

Some slaves said their owners hadn't been cruel. They ran away because they wanted to work for themselves and earn their own money. They wanted to raise their own families and live in peace. They didn't think anyone should own another person.

Sometimes small things make all the difference. Lewis Jones had worked hard for many years for his owner. Then one day Jones' aunt died. She was the only relative he had left. The owner wouldn't let Jones go to the funeral. He said there was no time to spare. That's when Lewis Jones decided to run away.

Some slaves simply said they'd rather die than stay a slave. And so they escaped.

Where would you first go when you ran away?

You might have to hide for days or weeks or even months before you found people to help you get to the North. Your owner would be searching for you, and so you would have to find secret hiding places.

Many slaves hid in forests and swamps. Some stayed in caves. Others hid in big trees.

You might have to hide in very uncomfortable places, like Hezekiah Hill did. For over a year he lived under the floor in a friend's house! His owner offered a big reward for Hill, but the slave hunters never found him.

Finally, after thirteen months, his friend found a boat that would take Hill to a northern city. The friend asked Hill to take along his seven-year-old son. The friend wanted his son to grow up a free man, even if it meant never seeing him again.

What dangers did you face?

The biggest danger was being caught. But there were many other dangers as well.

Wild animals lived in the forests and swamps. Alligators with jaws that were two feet long might snap at you. And you wouldn't want to run into a bear or a wild boar, or step on a poisonous snake.

One slave rode on a train heading north. He pretended to be a free black. Suddenly he saw his owner come into the car. The runaway jumped off the train, and his foot was crushed under the car wheels. When he finally arrived in Boston, doctors had to give him an artificial leg.

Slaves who ran away to the North were very brave. They suffered much pain and hunger along the way. Some of them even died before they made it. But those who reached the North said they would face the dangers all over again just to be free.

What would you eat while you were hiding?

You ate what you found — nuts, roots, berries, corn, and apples. You might catch fish or swamp rabbits. And now and then, if you were very careful, you might sneak into a farm at night and steal a pig or a chicken.

Most of the time you'd be too afraid to build a fire to cook. Someone might see the smoke.

Some runaway slaves solved the problem this way: They would build a small fire and then go off and hide. They would wait until the fire burned down to the coals and there was no smoke. Then it was safe to go back. They would cook the meat or fish quickly, wrap it in leaves, and move on to a new hiding place.

Where was the safest place to go?

Most runaway slaves went to the northern states. By 1800 slavery had ended in most of these states. The runaways fled to Philadelphia, Cincinnati, New York, Boston, and other cities and towns.

But in 1850 a new law made it unsafe even there. This law said that slave hunters could come into a northern state, find you, and say you had run away. Then they would handcuff you and take you back to the South.

And so you went even farther north — to Canada. The minute you set foot in Canada you were free. There is a story about a fugitive who was chased by his owner across the bridge from the United States to Canada. When he reached the Canadian side, he stopped suddenly. He turned around, looked the owner in the eye, and grinned. He was safe and free. They were equals now.

Slaves sang a song about Canada:

> O, old master, don't cry for me,
> For I am going to Canada
> Where colored men are free.

How would you hear about Canada?

Owners would tell their slaves that the North was a terrible place to live. They said the weather was cold, the land was difficult to farm, and the people were unfriendly. And they said that Canada was even worse.

Slaves pretended to believe this. They listened and nodded. But in their hearts they knew that if the owner said Canada was terrible, it must be wonderful.

Slaves learned about Canada in other ways, too. Those who lived for a while in the North and were brought back South spread the word. And some fugitives secretly came back to the South to help their friends and relatives escape. They told about their lives up north, and what it meant to be free.

How did owners try to catch the fugitives?

Most owners put advertisements in the newspapers when they discovered their slaves had escaped. The owners described the slaves and offered rewards for their capture. This is what some ads said:

$200 REWARD. Ran away, two **NEGRO MEN**, one, named Hanson, about forty years old, with one eye out, about 5 feet 4 inches in height. Whiskers. And Gusta is about 21 or 22 years and stoops in his walk.

Ranaway a Negro girl called Mary, has a small scar over her eye, a good many teeth missing, the letter **A** is branded on her cheek and forehead.

Did anyone help the owners?

Some people made their living by tracking fugitives. They were called slave hunters. Often an owner would hire a slave hunter to find a runaway slave.

Some hunters chased fugitives with dogs. The dog would smell a piece of clothing the slave had worn. Then it would be able to follow the trail for many miles. These dogs were called bloodhounds, and you can imagine why!

Sometimes hunters would break into homes looking for runaway slaves. They often kidnapped blacks from northern cities and took them to the South.

You could have been born free in New York and grown up there. But hunters could still kidnap you and sell you as a slave. This happened to Solomon Northup. He was taken to the South and kept as a slave for twelve years before he was able to prove he had been free.

Would you use disguises when you ran away?

There was a great danger that you might be caught. And so you would try not to look like yourself.

If you were a girl, you might put on pants and a shirt and a boy's hat. If you were a boy, you might wear a long dress with a high collar and a bonnet.

Sometimes you would pretend to be somebody else. One day three slaves who had saved some money got a coach and horses. They paid a poor white man to dress up as a southern gentleman. He sat inside the coach and they pretended to be his slaves. They carried his luggage and drove the coach all the way to the North.

Once a group of twenty-eight slaves escaped together. Hunters were hot on their trail. Friends who were helping the fugitives put them all in different carriages. Then they covered the carriages with black cloth and pretended they were driving to a funeral.

Everybody was very sad. They wiped their eyes and blew their noses. One of the slaves was *really* crying because her baby had died from the cold during the escape. The hunters never thought to stop the funeral carriages. And so the fugitives all drove to safety.

William and Ellen Craft were slaves who were married. After they escaped together, the newspapers in the North wrote stories about the disguises they had used. Ellen was very light-skinned. She dressed up as a white man and William pretended to be her slave.

Ellen cut her long hair. She wrapped a bandage around part of her face and wore a tall hat and dark glasses. She put her arm in a sling, pretending that it was broken. That way she wouldn't have to sign papers saying she was William's owner when she bought train tickets. She had to do this because she didn't know how to write.

The man sitting next to her on the train going north was her owner's neighbor, but he never recognized her!

Did you use special signals and codes on the Underground Railroad?

Everything about the Underground Railroad had to be a secret:
— who was a conductor,
— who ran a station house,
— when you would arrive at a station, and
— when you would leave for the next station.
Everyone who rode or worked on the Underground Railroad used secret codes to send information.

A certain number of knocks on the window or door in the middle of the night meant runaway slaves had arrived. If the station master asked, "Who's there?" the conductor might answer, "A friend with friends."

Often one station master would send a message to the next one saying that fugitives were coming. Of course, the message would be in code. "I have sent, at two o'clock, four large and two small hams." That meant that four grown-ups and two children would arrive on the two o'clock train.

You might have to travel from one station to the next without a conductor. If that happened, you usually had a password or special signal to look out for.

These were some of the Underground Railroad secret signals:

— In one city, slaves were told to go to the boat dock late at night. If they saw a man come off a certain boat and sprinkle ashes on the ground, it was safe to go on board.

— Illinois was a free state and Missouri had slaves. Students from an Illinois school would cross the Mississippi River on Sunday nights and go into Missouri. They walked along the shore and softly tapped stones together.

If you were hiding in the woods, you listened for the tapping. When you heard it, you came out. The students would lead you back across the river. They'd take you to a red barn that was an Underground Railroad station.

— In parts of Vermont, it was easy to find a station house. It had a row of bricks painted white around the chimney.

— Mrs. Piatt in Ohio invented one of the most unusual signals. Her husband was a judge and he followed the law. The law said you must not help fugitive slaves. But Mrs. Piatt felt slavery was wrong, and she wanted to do something about it.

The Piatts had a small statue in front of their house. When Judge Piatt was not home, the statue held a flag in its hand. This meant fugitives were welcome. When the flag was missing, it meant the Judge was home and you had to find another station.

How would you trick the slave hunters?

Hunters often used dogs to track you down. If they were hot on your trail, there was one trick you'd use if you could: walk as far as possible in a stream. The dogs couldn't smell your footprints in the water.

Some slaves taught themselves to read and write. Then they wrote out fake passes. Others borrowed a free black's papers and pretended to be that person. They would mail the papers back when they reached the North.

Some slave women would go on board a ship carrying clean, ironed shirts. Everybody thought they were bringing laundry to the sailors. Once on board, they hid and sailed to a northern port.

A number of fugitives traveled north in the most surprising way. They mailed themselves!

Henry Brown's story was so famous, his middle name became "Box." He mailed himself from Richmond, Virginia. He wrote on his box: "This Side Up."

But still he was turned upside down for many miles. When the box finally was opened in Philadelphia, Henry "Box" Brown stood up, reached out his hand, and said, "How do you do, gentlemen?"

Were there special hiding places on the Underground Railroad?

Many. There were secret attic rooms and fake closets. There were trapdoors and hidden tunnels that led to tiny rooms. In some houses you could push a button. A whole wall would then turn and you could hide behind it. There were sliding panels covered by pictures. Move the picture, push the panel, and you'd find a hiding place.

In one farmhouse, there was a secret room in the cellar. But you couldn't find the hiding place if you searched there. The only way to get to it was through a trap door from the room above. So many fugitives had hidden there that the house was called "Liberty Farm."

There were also secret compartments in the wagons you might travel in. One man built a false bottom on his cart. He put straw in the hidden bottom for fugitives to lie on. Then he filled the top part of the wagon with vegetables and drove off to the market.

How long would you stay at a station?

That depended on how close the hunters were. It might be two or three o'clock in the morning when you arrived at a friend's house. Sometimes there was barely time for the new conductor to get dressed. You would climb into a wagon with fresh horses and speed away to the next station ten or twenty miles away. The conductor had to return home in time for breakfast. That way everything looked normal. Conductors and station masters had to be very careful, because often many of their neighbors didn't believe in helping fugitive slaves. Some even thought slavery was all right.

Sometimes you might have to stay for a while at a station because you were sick.

Sarah Bradstreet was seven years old when a fugitive first came to her house. She held the lamp while her parents put medicine on his back. He was badly cut from having been whipped. It took two weeks before his wounds healed and he could travel to the next station.

Other times you might stay and work for several days or even weeks or months. The station master would hire you to do different jobs around the farm and house.

How long would the whole trip take?

The Underground Railroad ran in a zigzag way. The "tracks" couldn't go in a straight line because it would be too easy to catch the fugitives.

Safety was most important. Sometimes you had to head south to fool the hunters. They'd never think a runaway slave would go south. As soon as it was safe, you'd turn around and go back north.

It took one man a year to get from Alabama to Cincinnati, Ohio. Other fugitives were luckier. On board ship it might only take two or three days to get to a free state.

When was the best time of year to escape?

Some people said summer, some said winter.

If you traveled in summer, you didn't have to worry about the cold. The trees were green, and there were lots of berries and small animals for food. But it was also easier for the hunters to follow you.

Winter, of course, could be bitter cold. But there were good reasons for going then. The rivers were often frozen. You could cross them by walking on the ice. In the summer you might have to find a boat. Many slaves ran away at Christmas. Their owners were so busy going to parties, they might not notice for several days that a slave was missing. That would give you a head start.

Whether it was summer or winter, certain days were better than others for your escape. Saturday was best. The newspapers wouldn't print advertisements on Sunday. And so the owners couldn't tell everyone that you had run off. That also gave you a head start.

And whether it was summer or winter, you hoped for clear nights. Then you could look up at the sky and follow the North Star. It pointed toward freedom.

Who worked on the Underground Railroad?

All kinds of people. Blacks and whites, children and adults, women and men. There were Northerners, and also some Southerners who thought slavery was wrong and decided to help the fugitives.

Most of the people who helped were ordinary people — storekeepers, housewives, carpenters, ministers, teachers. We don't remember their names today.

But some conductors and station masters became very famous. Harriet Tubman was one. She had been a slave and escaped to the North. But she made trip after trip back to the South to help others escape. She was so successful that a reward of $40,000 was once offered to anyone who captured her. No one ever did.

Other blacks helped as well. By 1860 as many as 500 former slaves traveled every year from Canada back to the South to help rescue others.

And there were the Quakers. The Quakers were a religious group that was called the Society of Friends. The Friends believed that all people were equal. Their religion taught them that there should be no such thing as an owner and a slave. Many Quakers worked on the Underground Railroad. One famous Quaker station master was Thomas Garrett. Garrett helped nearly 3000 slaves to freedom, and not one was ever caught.

Not everyone worked as a conductor or station master. People helped in other ways. Some sewed new clothes for the slaves. Or collected money for food and medicine . . . or made speeches to tell people that slavery was wrong . . . or taught black children in schools . . . or even broke into jails to free captured slaves.

Sometimes you can know something is wrong but be too afraid to do anything. The people who worked on the Underground Railroad were very brave. They knew slavery was wrong. And they knew they could be put in prison for helping fugitives, or even killed. But they helped anyway.

How did people learn about the Underground Railroad?

In many ways — newspaper articles, speeches by runaway slaves, advertisements by owners trying to find their slaves, meetings of people working to help slaves. And a very famous book.

Harriet Beecher Stowe lived in Ohio and her house was a station on the Underground Railroad. But she did something even more important in the fight against slavery. She wrote a book called *Uncle Tom's Cabin.* In the 1850s people all over America and the world were talking about *Uncle Tom's Cabin.* Slave owners hated it. People who worked on the Underground Railroad loved it. Most of all, many people read it and for the first time thought about how terrible slavery was.

When Harriet Beecher Stowe visited the White House in 1863 at the time of the Civil War, it is said that President Abraham Lincoln met her and called her "the little woman who wrote the book that made this great war."

Was everyone in the North against slavery?

No. Slave hunters often paid people in the North for information about runaway slaves. Many Northerners even believed that white people had a right to own black people. Others were afraid that if blacks were free, they would take jobs that white people had.

Angry mobs sometimes broke up meetings where people were talking about the evils of slavery. Sometimes they would throw rotten eggs at the speakers. Other times they even burned down buildings and attacked people who were against slavery.

William Lloyd Garrison

William Lloyd Garrison published a newspaper called *The Liberator*. He wrote and printed articles against slavery. A gang of people attacked him in the streets of Boston one day. In order to protect him, the police put him in jail overnight. On the wall of the jail he wrote:

"William Lloyd Garrison was put into this cell on Monday afternoon, October 21, 1835, to save him from the violence of a . . . mob, who sought to destroy him for preaching . . . that all men are created equal."

How many slaves escaped?

No one really knows. Some say 35,000 and some say more than 100,000 slaves fled north.

Most people who worked on the Underground Railroad did not keep records of how many fugitives they helped. If the records were ever found, they could be punished for helping runaway slaves.

One man did keep records. His name was William Still and he was born a free black. He worked on the Underground Railroad in Philadelphia. During the Civil War, Still hid his records in a building at a cemetery. After the war was over, he published an 800-page book telling the stories of the hundreds of runaway slaves whom he had met and helped.

What happened if you were caught?

You were taken back to your owner and whipped. Some slaves were punished by having their feet put in heavy wooden frames called stocks so that they couldn't walk.

Some owners cut their slaves' feet so that they were crippled for life. That way they couldn't run away again.

When hunters chased slaves, they sometimes shot and wounded them. Some slaves were even killed.

Other times slaves killed themselves. They said they would rather be dead than go back to slavery.

Were people who helped you punished?

Yes. People who helped runaway slaves would pay a fine and sometimes be put in prison if they were caught. Some stayed in prison for many years. A few even died in prison.

One man who tried to help seven slaves escape was caught and put in jail. The letters "S.S." were branded on his hand. They stood for "Slave Stealer."

A whole group of families who lived in Berea, Kentucky, was forced to leave the state. They strongly believed slavery was wrong. One day men with rifles and guns rode into the town. They told these people they had to leave within ten days. Three days later, the families and their three church pastors packed up and moved to Ohio.

What did the Presidents of the United States think about the Underground Railroad?

Many Presidents before the Civil War believed that white Southerners had a right to own slaves. Some of the Presidents themselves, such as George Washington and Thomas Jefferson, owned slaves. They didn't believe people should help slaves escape from their owners.

But others thought slavery was wrong. One was Rutherford B. Hayes. Before he became President, Mr. Hayes was a lawyer in Ohio. In the 1850s he helped runaway slaves when their owners tried to take them back to the South.

What would you do when you became free?

One of the first things most slaves did was to change their names. They did this to be safe, but also for another reason.

Many slaves didn't have their own last names, but were given their owner's name. And so changing your name was as if you were throwing your owner out of your life. You were starting a new life, and it was a good way to get a fresh start.

Free blacks found jobs, earned money, and raised their families. Many wanted to learn to read and write, even though they were grown up.

Some secretly went back south and worked on the Underground Railroad, helping other blacks to escape. Sometimes they were able to bring families together after many years.

This happened to William Still, the free black who worked on the Underground Railroad in Philadelphia. One day he met a man in the street who had just escaped from the South. They talked for a while and William discovered the man was his long-lost brother Peter! They had never met before. Peter was six years old when he was sold. Their mother had escaped to the North and William was born there. The Underground Railroad brought the two brothers together.

Most of all, the fugitives felt happy to be free. When he was told he was free, Tom Robinson said:

"Was I happy? You can take anything. No matter how good you treat it — it wants to be free. You can treat it good and feed it good and give it everything it seems to want — but if you open the cage — it's happy."

When did the Underground Railroad stop running?

On December 18, 1865, at the end of the Civil War, the Constitution of the United States was changed to say that slavery was ended forever.

Some people believe that the Underground Railroad itself was very important in ending slavery. People in the southern states were very angry about all the escapes. The greatest number of slaves had escaped just before the Civil War started.

When the war ended, slavery ended. And the Underground Railroad ended as well. When you no longer had to escape to be free, then you didn't need an Underground Railroad anymore.

Would you like to know more about the Underground Railroad? Here are some museums you and your family may want to visit.

National Underground Railroad
Freedom Center
50 East Freedom Way
Cincinnati, OH 45202
Telephone: 877-648-4838
www.freedomcenter.org

Slave Haven Underground Railroad Museum
826 N. Second Street
Memphis, TN 38107
Telephone: 901-527-3427

Reginald F. Lewis Museum of
Maryland African American History & Culture
830 E. Pratt Street
Baltimore, MD 21202
Telephone: 443-263-1800
www.africanamericanculture.org

Charles H. Wright Museum of African American History
315 E. Warren Avenue
Detroit, MI 48201-1443
Telephone: 313-494-5800
www.maah-detroit.org

As of Summer 2005, large museums in Charleston, SC; Fredericksburg, VA; and Baltimore, MD, are under construction. One is also planned for the National Mall in Washington, D.C.

Special Event: Log on to www.stealawaytofreedom.com for information about the annual Steal Away to Freedom Weekend held every July in upstate New York. The weekend includes storytellers, performers, seminars, and tours of Underground Railroad safe houses.